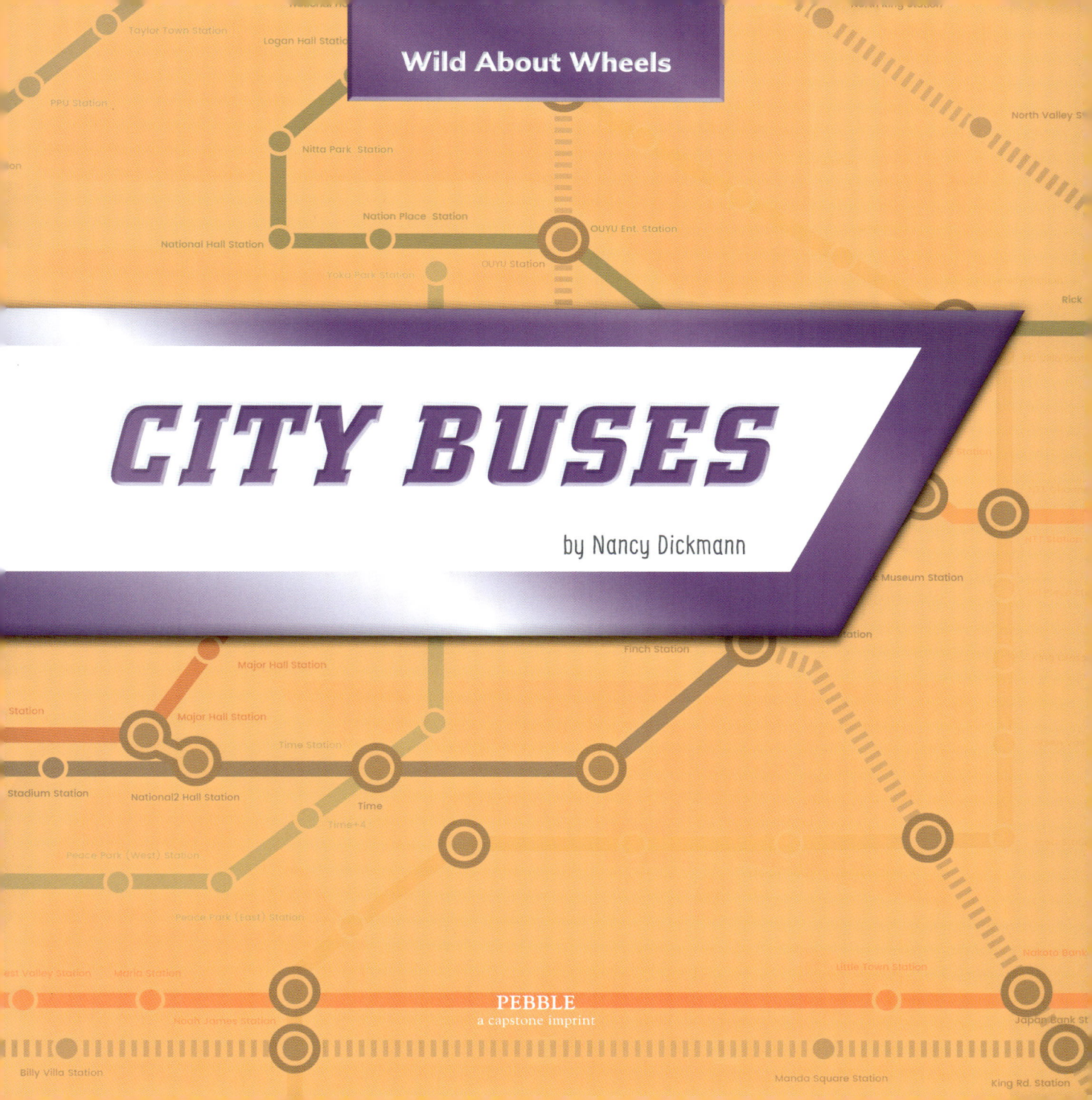

Wild About Wheels

CITY BUSES

by Nancy Dickmann

PEBBLE
a capstone imprint

Pebble Emerge is published by Pebble, an imprint of Capstone.
1710 Roe Crest Drive
North Mankato, Minnesota 56003
www.capstonepub.com

Copyright © 2022 by Capstone. All rights reserved. No part of this publication may be reproduced in whole or in part, or stored in a retrieval system, or transmitted in any form or by any means, electronic, mechanical, photocopying, recording, or otherwise, without written permission of the publisher.

Library of Congress Cataloging-in-Publication Data
Names: Dickmann, Nancy, author.
Title: City buses / by Nancy Dickmann.
Description: North Mankato, Minnesota : Pebble, [2022] | Series: Wild about wheels | Includes bibliographical references and index. | Audience: Ages 6-8 | Audience: Grades 2-3 | Summary: "You need to get to another part of a big city quickly. What can you do? Take the city bus! City buses take people where they need to go day after day. They help people get to workplaces, stores, and more. They are hard at work in all types of weather. Young readers will learn about the main parts of city buses, how they work, and why they are important to cities and the people who ride them"-- Provided by publisher.
Identifiers: LCCN 2020025528 (print) | LCCN 2020025529 (ebook) |
 ISBN 9781977132321 (hardcover) | ISBN 9781977133267 (paperback) |
 ISBN 9781977154026 (ebook pdf)
Subjects: LCSH: Buses--Juvenile literature. | Bus rapid transit--Juvenile literature.
Classification: LCC TL232 .D53 2022 (print) | LCC TL232 (ebook) | DDC 388.3/4233--dc23
LC record available at https://lccn.loc.gov/2020025528
LC ebook record available at https://lccn.loc.gov/2020025529

Image Credits
Alamy: keith morris, 17, Wild Places Photography/Chris Howes, 16; Capstone Studio: Karon Dubke, 21 (back); Getty Images: Anadolu Agency/Ali Atmaca, 8; iStockphoto: anilbolukbas, 10, BDMcIntosh, cover, back cover, Drazen, 9; Shutterstock: Ander Dylan, 14, Andrew V Marcus, 18–19, Bikeworldtravel, 11, dade72, 5, Dusan Petkovic, 7, istanbulphotos, 6, Pavel L Photo and Video, 13, RaksyBH, 15, Rawpixel (background), throughout, Snamenski, 21 (front), vaalaa, 12, William Perugini, 4

Editorial Credits
Editor: Amy McDonald Maranville; Designer: Cynthia Della-Rovere; Media Researcher: Eric Gohl; Production Specialist: Katy LaVigne

All internet sites appearing in back matter were available and accurate when this book was sent to press.

Printed in the United States   4878

Table of Contents

What City Buses Do 4

Look Inside. 8

Look Outside. 14

    City Bus Diagram 18

    Plan a Bus Route 20

    Glossary 22

    Read More 23

    Internet Sites 23

    Index 24

Words in **bold** are in the glossary.

What City Buses Do

You want to go to the library with your family in a big city. It's too far to walk. How can you get there? You can take the bus!

Anyone can ride a city bus. The people riding are called **passengers**. They get on and pay their **fare**. The bus makes lots of stops. Passengers get on and off.

City buses take people where they want to go. Not everyone has a car. Buses help them get to work or school.

A bus can carry many people. These people do not need to drive cars. Gas-powered cars **pollute** the air. With fewer of them, there is less pollution.

Look Inside

The driver sits in the front. There are pedals and a steering wheel. The driver uses them to drive. There are controls to open the doors.

There are different ways to pay the fare. Sometimes you buy a ticket before you get on. You might hand money to the driver. You can even tap a **pass** on a **card reader**.

A bus has lots of seats. Sometimes the bus is very full. Passengers have to stand. They can hold on to bars or straps.

There are buttons by some of the seats. You can push the button. This tells the driver you want to get off. Some buses have a cord to pull instead.

This bus has an **engine** that uses **diesel** fuel. It can cause pollution. Electric buses are cleaner. They have a **battery** and an electric motor inside. The battery needs to be recharged when its power runs low.

A hybrid bus has an electric motor and a diesel engine. The bus uses the electric motor. It can use the diesel engine when the battery needs to recharge.

Look Outside

Many buses have a ramp. A wheelchair can drive up. When the chair is inside, the doors can close.

Each bus has a sign on the front.
Sometimes there is a sign on the side too.
The sign tells people the **route** number.
It tells people where the bus will go.

Many buses run day and night. Buses have headlights. They help the driver see when it is dark. They help other drivers see the bus too.

Buses run in all kinds of weather. They have windshield wipers that wipe the rain away. Now the driver can see the road. The bus can drive safely.

City Bus Diagram

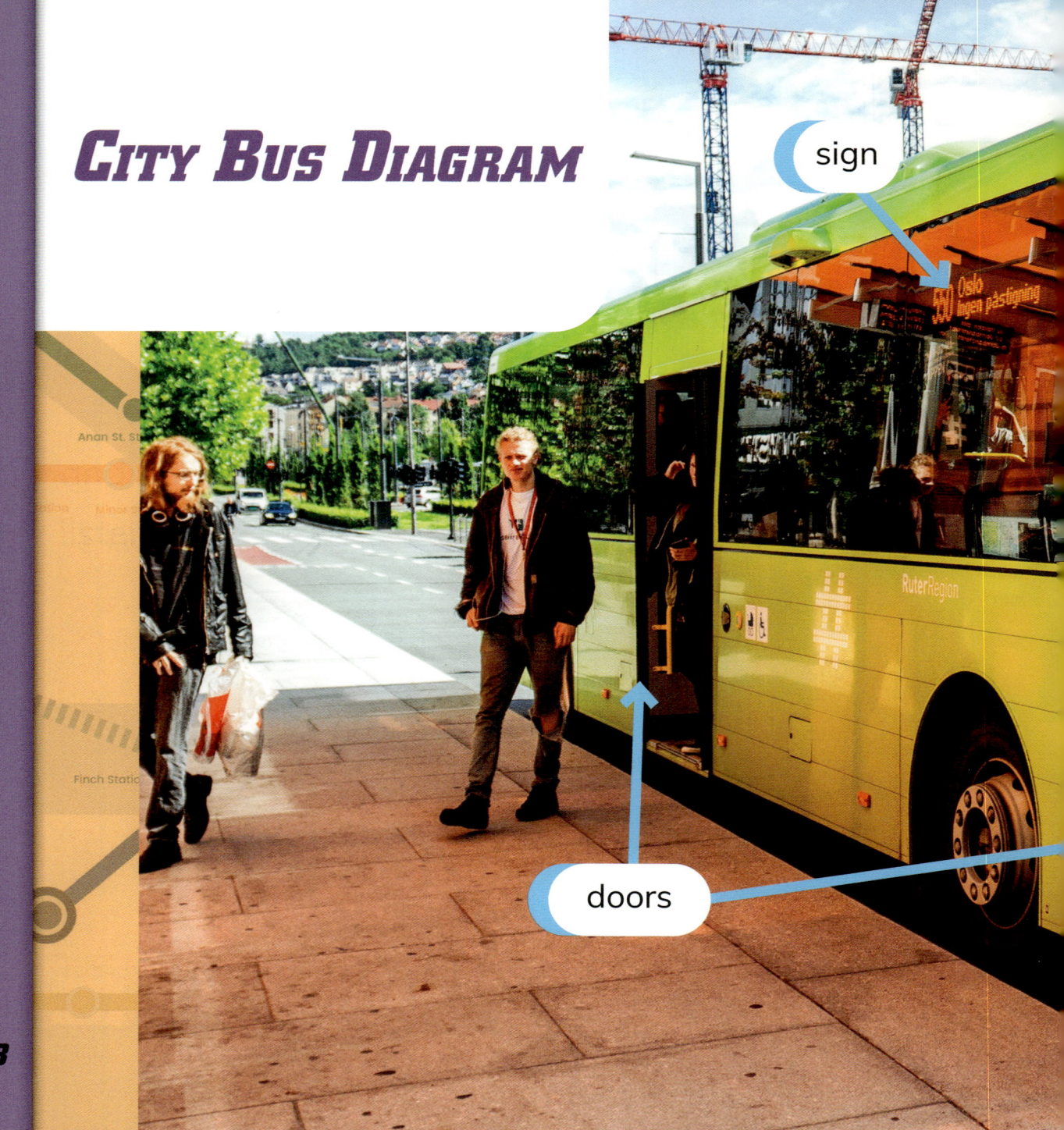

sign

doors

18

sign

wipers

headlights

19

Plan a Bus Route

Imagine you are in charge of a city bus. Where would it go? You can find a map of your neighborhood and copy it. Or you can draw one yourself. Label stores, schools, and parks. Now plan a route. Where would a bus be most useful? Where will you put the bus stops? Draw them on your map.

North King Station

21

Glossary

battery (BAT-ur-ee)—a container filled with chemicals that produces electrical power

card reader (KARD REED-ur)—a machine that reads and checks an electronic pass

diesel (DEE-zul)—a type of fuel that is made from oil

engine (EN-jin)—a machine that makes the power needed to move something

fare (FAIR)—money that a passenger must pay to ride a bus or other vehicle

pass (PASS)—a card that allows a person to ride a bus

passenger (PASS-en-jer)—a person who rides a bus, train, or other vehicle

pollute (pu-LOOT)—to make the air, land, or water dirty

route (ROOT)—the road or course followed to get somewhere

Read More

Mattern, Joanne. *We Go on a City Bus*. Egremont, MA: Red Chair Press, 2019.

Meister, Cari. *Buses*. North Mankato, MN: Pebble, 2019.

Rustad, Martha. *Transportation in Many Cultures*. North Mankato, MN: Capstone Press, 2016.

Internet Sites

Easy Science for Kids: Transportation
easyscienceforkids.com/all-about-transportation/

Kiddle: Bus Facts for Kids
kids.kiddle.co/Bus

Index

bars, 10
batteries, 12, 13
buttons, 11

card readers, 9
cars, 6, 7
cords, 11

doors, 8, 14
drivers, 8, 9, 11, 16, 17

electric motors, 12, 13
engines, 12, 13

fares, 5, 9

headlights, 16

passengers, 5, 10
passes, 9
pedals, 8
pollution, 7, 12

rain, 17
ramps, 14
routes, 15

seats, 10, 11
signs, 15
steering wheels, 8
straps, 10

wheelchairs, 14
windshield wipers, 17